TRACK & FIELD
TRAINING AND FITNESS

MORGAN HUGHES

The Rourke Press, Inc.
Vero Beach, Florida 32964

Morgan Hughes is a sports writer who has covered professional hockey, baseball, tennis and cycling. He has written several childrens books, both fiction and nonfiction, and is currently at work on his first full-length novel.

PROJECT ADVISOR:
Richard Roberts is the former head track and field coach at Florida State University, where he was also a star athlete during his undergraduate studies. He resides in Tallahassee with his wife and three hunting dogs.

PHOTO CREDITS:
All photos by Ryals Lee, Jr., except: Victah Sailer (page 39); Morgan Hughes (page 4, 26, 40, 42, 43)

ILLUSTRATIONS:
Jon DiVenti, Kingfish Studio (page 16)
Matt Willard, Kingfish Studio (page 23, 27, 31, 34)

EDITORIAL SERVICES: Janice L. Smith for Penworthy

Library of Congress Cataloging-in-Publication Data

Hughes, Morgan, 1957-
    Track and field / Morgan E. Hughes.
       p. cm.
    Include indexes.
    Contents: [1] An Introduction to Track & Field — [2] The sprints — [3] Middle and long distance runs — [4] The jumps — [5] The throws — [6] Training and fitness.
       ISBN 1-57103-288-6 (v. 1). — ISBN 1-57103-291-6 (v. 2). — ISBN 1-57103-289-4 (v. 3). — ISBN 1-57103-290-8 (v. 4). — ISBN 1-57103-292-4 (v. 5). — ISBN 1-57103-293-2 (v. 6)
    1. Track-athletics Juvenile literature. [1. Track and field.] I. Title.
GV1060.5.H833 1999
796.42—dc21   99-20284
                                                                      CIP

Printed in the USA

TABLE OF CONTENTS

It's never too early to begin a career in track and field.

CHAPTER ONE

BUILDING STRENGTH

By participating in organized sports—such as track and field—you, the young athlete, will give yourself the chance not only to get in shape, but to stay in shape and build good health habits that can last a lifetime.

With the help of your coaches and parents, you'll create workout programs to build strength and increase **flexibility.** Further, you will learn eating habits which aim to minimize your intake of "junk" foods and replace them with nutritious—and good tasting—meals. You'll learn that "good for you" doesn't necessarily mean "tastes bad."

There are several "principles" of successful training you should keep in mind. These fundamental rules can help you avoid injuries and frustrating setbacks.

First, as you begin a new training program, learn to let your body **adapt** to new stresses and strains. When you start training, whether you're throwing a javelin or running hurdles, you may experience some unfamiliar aches and pains. With careful stretching you can keep these "normal" aches from becoming injuries.

Second, don't overdo it. For example, when you begin training for the 100-meter dash, you should work slowly to the stage where you can burst out of the starting blocks and into a full sprint without risking injury (muscle pulls, ligament tears, etc.). Then, limit the number of sprints you run during a given workout. If you do too much today, you may not be able to do anything tomorrow.

★ DID YOU KNOW?

While the ancient Egyptians and Persians used physical training for military reasons, the Greeks viewed good health as a pathway to becoming a better all-around person.

A sprinter has to work gradually toward full speed.

There are all kinds of exercises for agility and strength.

Third, with the help of your coach, learn to increase your **exertion** gradually. Your goal is to train your heart to pump the same amount of blood with fewer actual beats.

Depending on which events you decide to try—anything from the high jump to the shot put—you will also have to spend time training specifically for that event. No matter what event or events you choose, and no matter how much natural talent and physical fitness you possess, you can become truly skilled (that is, ready to compete) only through carefully supervised practice.

For example, if you want to run the hurdles, you will have to complete all the stretching exercises to safeguard against injuries, but then you'll also have to spend a good deal of time going through the specific motions unique to hurdles, to teach your body how to do it.

Have you ever heard the term **muscle memory**? Well, this is it. You actually have to teach your specific muscle groups to perform so they won't have to think about what to do on the day of competition.

★ **DID YOU KNOW?**

Muscles do many things: help move the body's limbs, pump blood, and draw air into the lungs. While you teach your muscles through exercise, take time to learn more about them, too.

Every sports activity requires fundamental physical strength. Without basic muscular energy you can't even begin to develop **endurance**, or the capability to continue even during strenuous activity. However, you need more than simple muscle strength. Track and field athletes are not bodybuilders after all. Rather, track and field athletes are strong, but they are also graceful, often slim, athletes whose bodies are carefully built for speed, agility, and **stamina**.

Your coach plays an important role in designing the workout/training schedule that will help you develop the muscle memory you need to compete.

Track athletes tend to be very lean.

If you don't stretch before you train, you may suffer injuries.

Your coach will help you avoid "bulking up," or becoming muscle-bound. This may look good at the beach, but for some events this strategy can only lead to injury and/or poor performances.

One of the most important steps every young athlete should take before beginning any training program in any sport is to visit the doctor for a complete physical exam.

This is important for several reasons. First, a qualified doctor may discover problems or conditions which could prevent you, as a young athlete, from achieving your goals. Second, during a pre-training exam, your doctor may gather information about your general health and fitness which will help you design your specific workout program. Lastly, no young athlete-in-training should run the risk of falling victim to an illness or condition which could have been detected and treated earlier.

IMPROVED FLEXIBILITY

Most track and field athletes compete in "fast" events. The dashes, the jumps, and the throws all require explosive body functions. In order to protect the body's various muscles, ligaments, and **tendons** from injury during these demanding events, it's crucial that you warm up properly.

Vigorous activity itself causes unavoidable muscle injury simply because as muscles heat up, they become shorter and tighter. However, a few minutes of proper stretching before training or competing can prevent weeks, even months, of rehabilitation from painful injuries.

Stretching is one of the most important elements of a proper warm-up. Many injuries occur to the legs—strained calf muscles, pulled hamstrings, pulled groins, and torn **Achilles tendons.** The risk of these injuries can be reduced with improved flexibility.

A growing number of coaches across the country are recommending that their athletes stretch both before and after training sessions and competitions.

The first rule of proper stretching is to start slowly. You can do as much damage by overstretching in warm-ups as you can by dashing out onto the track or hurling a javelin with no warm-up at all.

★ DID YOU KNOW?

Muscle tissue is basically stretchy. But through careful exercise, you can increase the length of your muscles, which is how you become more flexible.

COMMON ATHLETIC INJURIES

BLISTERS: Always be sure your shoes are the right size for your feet. Try wearing two pairs of socks. Alcohol and a bandage will help keep a blister from breaking. If it does, wash it well and apply alcohol in a 70% solution to stop infection.

FOOT SPRAIN: Make sure your shoes have a good arch support and thick, flexible soles to absorb shock. Use a heel pad if you feel pain there. Use ice to reduce swelling.

ANKLE SPRAIN: In addition to making sure your shoes fit properly, always take the time to stretch before exercise. Ice any injury for 30 minutes and use an elastic bandage to help limit swelling. If necessary, have a doctor look for fractures.

KNEE SPRAIN: Correctly fitted shoes are vital, as well as avoiding certain very stressful activities (full squats). Try to exercise on level ground and don't run downhill if you can walk instead. Ice any injury and try to keep your weight off it until the pain is significantly reduced.

SHIN SPLINTS: Stretch diligently to strengthen the shin muscles and develop more flexibility in the ankles. Sprinters should avoid sudden stops. Massage with ice may help. If the pain persists, a doctor must be consulted.

PULLS, STRAINS, BRUISES: Stretching is the best insurance policy, in addition to using the right equipment (right size, etc.). Ice any injured area for 30 minutes and wrap in an elastic bandage to help limit swelling. Avoid putting weight on the area until pain is significantly reduced.

CRAMPS: Always pay attention to signs of fatigue which can lead to cramps. Drink plenty of liquids to avoid dehydration. If you suffer cramps, stop all activity and slowly massage any affected area. Careful stretching also helps loosen cramps.

HAMSTRINGS: Your legs are your lifeline in track and field, so take care of them with dedication to stretching and proper warm-ups. If you get tired, stop. Don't extend to the point of causing yourself time-wasting injuries.

Many common athletic injuries can be prevented.

Stretching exercises are an essential part of warm-ups.

16

The following exercises will help guard against injury. They should be performed before every training session and competition. Most coaches agree that warm-ups should be completed 15-20 minutes before the start of training or competition to allow the stretched muscles to relax—but not to be too tired from the warm-up itself. Remember, go slowly, hold your stretch positions the proper amount of time (**static stretching**), and never bounce (ballistic stretching)!

Static stretching means that when you reach your fully stretched position, you should hold that position for a count of up to ten (without bouncing), then relax. This technique should be used with all stretching exercises.

Toe touches warm up and stretch the hamstrings, which are the large muscles in the back of the thigh. In a sitting position with your legs extended, place your heels together and knees straight (but not locked). Then bend over slowly and reach for your toes. Hold this position for 10-15 seconds, then slowly straighten up. Repeat 5-10 times.

Trunk twisters are designed to loosen up the spinal vertebrae and are simple to perform. Sit on a stool with your feet shoulders-width apart and your hands on your hips. Twist as far as you can one way, hold the position for a count of five, then twist the opposite way. Make your motion smooth and avoid any jerking which might cause injury.

> ★ **DID YOU KNOW?**
>
> Isotonic contractions occur when muscles tighten (contract) and there is visible movement. Isometric contractions occur when the muscles tighten but there is no visible movement.

Quad stretches warm the muscles in the front of the thigh (quadriceps). While standing, hold a chair for support. Lift one foot and grasp it, pulling it close to your buttock. Hold for a count of five, then release and repeat with the other leg.

Achilles stretches are very important as injuries to this tendon are extremely painful and slow to heal. Stand facing a wall with your hands shoulders-width apart and flat on the wall. Your feet should be three to four feet (one meter) from the wall. Keeping your heels flat on the floor, slowly bend your elbows to bring your upper body closer to the wall. This will stretch the Achilles tendons on both legs.

Use whatever objects you need to complete your warm-ups.

Some warm-up exercises look "funny" but serve an important purpose.

Hurdlers' stretches help loosen the groin and leg muscles. Sit on the floor, point one leg forward, and bend the other leg behind you with the foot resting near your buttocks. Slowly reach for the toes of the extended foot and hold. Then repeat with the other leg.

Your coach will provide many other basic stretching exercises. Keep in mind the importance of doing these drills slowly and correctly. There is nothing to be gained by hurrying them. If you rush through or skip warm-ups you will only increase your chances of injury.

Remember, muscles often come in pairs. For example, you have one muscle that bends the knee and a different one that straightens it. The same principle applies to most muscles in your body. So, as you warm up one set of muscles, make sure you give the "opposite" muscle the same benefit of stretching. You'll feel better and you'll perform better when competition (or training) begins.

CHAPTER THREE

INCREASED ENDURANCE

Have you ever noticed the differences in body type between sprinters and marathon runners? Both are runners, but the similarity ends there. Sprinters tend to be muscular—powerfully built—while their long-distance counterparts, the cross-country specialists, are lean and wiry—though their athletic accomplishments are among the most awe-inspiring in all sports.

Just as there are many different body types in the world of track and field, so are there many kinds of training, depending on which event you choose.

Building endurance is vital for most track and field athletes, even though the sprint races (including the shorter hurdling events) call for "training" endurance rather than "competition" endurance.

Be patient when you start a new training program. Even if you're healthy and in reasonably good shape, you will probably tire quickly in the first days and weeks of your training. Like the skills you're working so hard to develop, it will take time for your endurance to build, but rest assured that it will.

The basic focus of endurance training is to develop **cardiovascular** endurance. This allows you to take in large quantities of oxygen when you inhale and expend equally

hen the heart and lungs are strong and working well together, the oxygen in the blood can be carried to the muscles more efficiently. Muscular endurance, which allows athletes to continue to compete at a high level even when they may be exhausted from their exertions, is different.

★ DID YOU KNOW?

Endurance is closely linked to strength. As a muscle becomes strong, it usually develops more endurance as well. That is, it is capable of more repetitions of a particular activity.

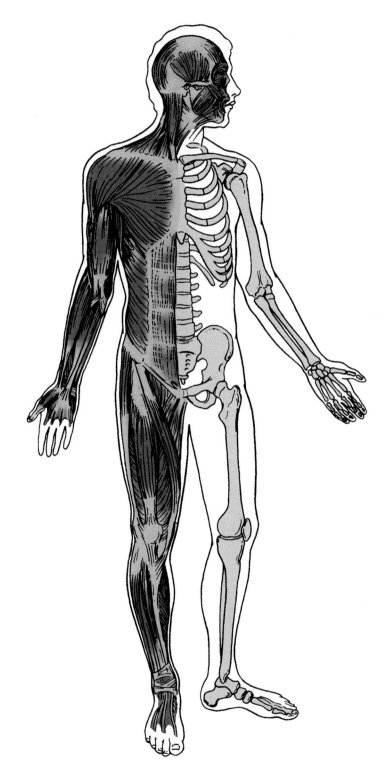

The musculoskeletal system is a complex network of muscles and bones.

A hurdler needs "fast twitch" fibers.

Muscles are made up of two kinds of fibers, called **"fast twitch" fibers** and **"slow twitch" fibers**. Scientists have looked at both kinds of fibers under microscopes and found that "slow" twitch fibers are red because they are rich in blood. These fibers function well in endurance activities (like cross-country running).

The "fast" twitch fibers look white under the microscope because they are not rich in blood. These fibers function well for speed and power. They come into play in all the short sprint events, as well as in the high impact events like shot put, discus, javelin, and the jumps.

Every human being is born with a unique balance of fast-to-slow twitch fibers. This ratio cannot be significantly changed. On the other hand, through training, each kind of fiber can be helped to perform to the maximum level.

Training for endurance is your way of warding off the natural effects of fatigue. You can gain endurance by training your muscles "just a little more" than you'll need to for competition. If you race in the 1,500 meters, you might include some 3,000-meter runs in your training program. This common practice is called over-distance training.

★ DID YOU KNOW?

When a person stops exercising, the muscles may begin to atrophy, which means they lose both strength and endurance. It's vital to maintain tone through consistent exercise.

25

The Importance of Rest

No matter how enthusiastic you are, how strong you feel, and how anxious you are to improve, it's important to listen to your coaches when they tell you to rest.

Your muscles contain a stored energy source called **glycogen,** which is a kind of fuel. When you compete or work out at a strenuous level, you use up your stores of glycogen and potassium. It can take as long as two days for your levels to return to normal. (One hint for getting potassium back into your system—eat bananas!)

Your coach will help you apply your enthusiasm without overdoing it.

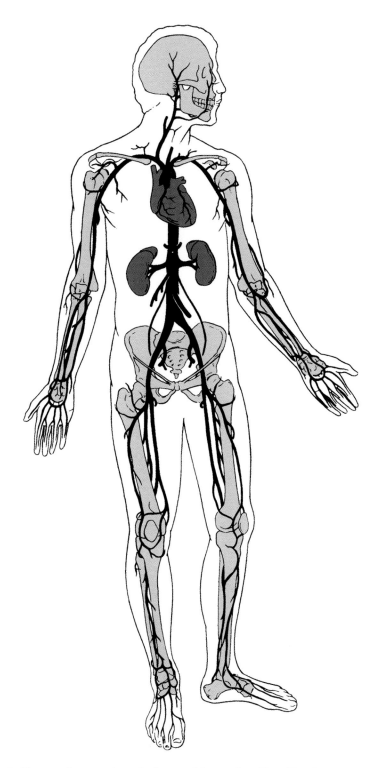

The arterial/vascular system helps athletes by distributing oxygen-rich blood throughout the body.

Hard-Easy Principle of Training—Avoid Overtraining

If you find that you're tired all the time, your mood is often cranky, your joints are stiff and your muscles are sore, there is a good chance you are the victim of "too much of a good thing." Training is the "good thing." But **overtraining** isn't. In fact, most coaches, trainers, and **physiologists** agree overtraining is as bad for you as not training at all.

Again, heed the advice of your coaches and make rest and recovery an important part of your program. You can't make the most of your talents if you don't maintain a balance. Your dedication to training will be rewarded with good results. If you exercise common sense (by exercising sensibly!) you will be rewarded with the good health and fitness necessary to compete in the first place.

CHAPTER FOUR

PROPER NUTRITION

One of the simplest and most important factors of successful competition is good health. And good health relies heavily on proper diet and nutrition.

In the computer industry, there is a saying "Garbage in, garbage out." It means that what eventually comes out of a computer depends greatly on what goes into the computer at the programming stage.

The same is true for the competitive athlete. Whatever you put into your body in terms of food and nutrition will have an impact on how your body performs when it is time to train and compete.

As an athlete it's very important to watch what you eat. Unfortunately, this means eliminating much of the fast-food or other "junk" food that may be part of your diet. And always make sure your diet includes the recommended amounts of the four basic elements: **protein**, carbohydrates, fats, and fiber.

Protein

In recent years, protein has taken on a bad name among those health experts who believe people ingest too much unnecessary protein. In the right amount, protein is a vital life source. It can be found in cheese, eggs, meat, and fish. Proteins are important for body development and for healing tired or injured muscles.

Some proteins—such as those found in red meat—take a long time to digest and should be carefully planned into your diet. The traditional pregame meal of meat and potatoes has been rejected by most modern nutrition experts. Carbohydrates such as rice, pasta, and bread are more easily turned into fuel.

★ DID YOU KNOW?

The body burns more calories during physical activity than when at rest, which is why "couch potatoes" run the risk of becoming overweight while athletes remain trim.

Meats and cheeses are important sources of protein.

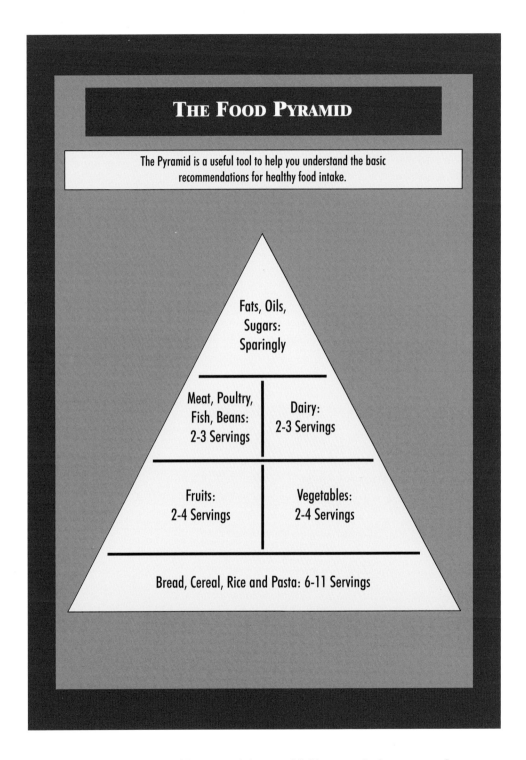

THE FOOD PYRAMID

The Pyramid is a useful tool to help you understand the basic recommendations for healthy food intake.

Fats, Oils, Sugars: Sparingly

Meat, Poultry, Fish, Beans: 2-3 Servings

Dairy: 2-3 Servings

Fruits: 2-4 Servings

Vegetables: 2-4 Servings

Bread, Cereal, Rice and Pasta: 6-11 Servings

The Food Pyramid provides nutrition guidelines to help you make good choices.

Carbohydrates

For athletes, carbohydrates are the primary source of energy. High in oxygen, hydrogen, and carbon, they include all the sugars and starches. You may think of sugar as something you spoon onto breakfast cereal, but there are several different kinds of sugars. For example, fructose is found in ripe fruit, honey, and many vegetables. On the other hand, lactose is a sugar found in milk. Maltose comes from digested starch or malt, and sucrose, the most common table sugar, is derived from sugar cane, beets, maple syrup, and sorghum.

Starches are found in such foods as potatoes, peas, beans, nuts, carrots, beets, and cereal grains (oats, corn, barley, rye, rice, and wheat). Carbohydrates are particularly important on "game" day when your body is working its hardest and using up stored energy at its fastest rate. Because carbohydrates go into the body easily, they are also used up quickly and must be restocked. Thus a "high-carb" diet is not a bad thing for an active person.

★ DID YOU KNOW?

An active person's diet might consist of 60-70% carbohydrates, 10-20% protein, and 15-20% fat—although it's a good idea to talk to your doctor or a nutritional expert for a more personalized plan.

Fats

Many so-called "energy foods" fall into the category of fats. They should not be entirely ignored, but their intake should be carefully monitored. Some "fats" include butter, vegetable oils, selected meats (typically red meat), and the wide array of "sweets"—cookies, candy, cake, ice cream, etc.—that are so appealing to many youngsters.

Your body needs some of these elements for maximum all-around health, but it is important to keep fats to a minimal level.

Eating multiple servings of fruits and vegetables daily will help keep you fit.

THINK BEFORE YOU SNACK

Everybody loves a snack in the middle of the day or when they feel their energy level begin to wane. But you should be careful what you eat.

FOOD ITEM	CALORIES
Popcorn (1 cup)	55
Doughnut (1)	75
Fruit (2 servings)	100
Nuts (20)	100
Chocolate Bars (1 small bar)	150
Milk (8 oz)	175
Potato Chips (20)	200
Bread (2 servings)	250
Cookies (5)	250
French Fries (20)	250
Ice Cream Soda (1)	260
Fudge Sundae (1)	350
Ice Cream (1 cup)	400
Cheeseburger (1)	400
Meat (6 oz)	450

Be aware of the calories contained in common snack foods and choose wisely.

Fiber

The last category is fiber (which used to be called cellulose). Here you'll find most vegetables and fruits. These food items are vital for healthy digestion and keep the body's internal plumbing free flowing and clear of obstacles. There is almost no limit to the amount of these foods that an active person (i.e., an athlete) may consume.

Many doctors agree that it is more beneficial to go "directly to the source." For example, at breakfast, don't settle for a glass of orange juice; instead eat the orange, which gives you all the fiber you need as well as the vitamins from the juice. See the chart on page 35 for some examples of high- and low-calorie food items you may have in your diet.

CHAPTER FIVE

THE MENTAL GAME

Believe it or not, participating in sports—such as track and field—isn't just good for the body. It's also very good for the mind. Studies have shown that physical activity has a direct positive correlation on a person's ability to learn.

Other studies have determined that physical activities are a wonderful way to release emotional tension.

Furthermore, a person's self-image may improve, along with his or her confidence and ability to perform in stressful situations (like taking a test in school).

It's nice to know that doing something that is fun, such as participating in organized sports, is also good for you. But there's more to it than that.

Young athletes must also wrestle with age-old values about winning and losing and then decide individually how important the glory is. The old adage says, "Winning isn't everything, it's the only thing. Losing isn't just bad, it's unforgivable." There are also those who may claim that mere sportsmanship—the respect you show to your opponents, even if they've just beaten you—is a phony waste of time. Don't believe it.

Winning in sports is important. However, it isn't a matter of life and death. The issue of winning and losing teaches us valuable lessons about how our society works. That is, some days you succeed and other days you fail. But always, life goes on.

A rock 'n' roll song from the 1990s included the lyrics, "Sometimes you're the windshield. Sometimes you're the bug. On the field of play, you'll know both glory and defeat."

DID YOU KNOW?

For any athlete, especially young ones, it's extremely critical to minimize the risk of minor injuries (blisters, sprains, strains, and shin splints) as well as major ones (broken bones, muscle tears).

Athletics help to build friendships and a sense of teamwork.

Don't stand on the sidelines ... get involved!

Have Fun, Don't Worry

The most important element of sports for every young athlete is the factor of fun. When you're older—in high school or college—you can worry about becoming a champion. For now, you should concentrate on having fun.

For example, you shouldn't play soccer just because your best buddy plays soccer—unless you like the game as much as he or she does. Nor should you take up track and field just because your mother or father tells you it's good for you. In order to get something out of the experience, you have to enjoy it.

Remember this basic rule: You should want to go to practice every day. If you have to be dragged kicking and yelling to the practice field, you're in the wrong sport. In this case, look around for a new dream to pursue.

Simple, basic enjoyment of an activity should never be underestimated. The "fun" of playing a sport is the glue that helps you stick with it during the low points.

★ **DID YOU KNOW?**

No matter how much enthusiasm you bring to sports, you'll still run into frustrations. Don't let them get the best of you. With the help of your parents and coach, focus on fun and steady improvement.

Play for the Enjoyment of the Game, Not for Your Parents

Experts in the field of child psychology agree that many promising young athletes suffer from "burn out" by the time they reach their teen years because of the years of pressure to win placed on them by their parents. Of course, this is a tricky business. Our parents are, at once, our most loyal supporters and most demanding critics.

Try new events—you may be surprised at how good you are at them.

Remember the most important aspect of sports is to have fun!

When you step on the field of play, the only person who can control your performance is you (and perhaps your coach). If you set out with the goal of pleasing someone else, you may end up very disappointed. It is important to have a cause rather than a selfish motive.

There are many reasons to get involved in organized sports. Some kids join teams simply to have fun, while others want to improve the skills they already have and learn new ones. Some boys and girls may get involved in athletics to be with their friends in a "special" environment, or to make new friends and see new sights.

Some kids may view sports as a chance to experience the thrill of victory, while others see it as a way simply to improve their physical fitness.

Whatever your reasons, make sure you find an activity you really like. It will make all the difference when you move past the introductory stage and get down to the nitty gritty.

Good luck and have fun!

GLOSSARY

Achilles tendon (uh KIL eez TEN dun) — the large tendon running from the heel bone to the calf muscle

adapt (uh DAPT) — to adjust to a new circumstance

cardiovascular (KAHRD ee o VAS kyoo lur) — relating to the heart and blood vessels

endurance (in DER uns) — the ability of an individual to resist the effects of adversity (in this case physical adversity)

exertion (ig ZER shun) — a strenuous or vigorous physical effort

fast twitch fibers (FAST TWICH FIE berz) — muscular fibers which help with high-impact activities (sprinting, jumping, etc.)

flexibility (FLEK suh BIL ut ee) — the ability of an individual to bend, turn and twist beyond normal range

glycogen (GLIE kuh jen) — a white, sweet-tasting powder, found in the liver, which acts as a storage carbohydrate

muscle memory (MUS l MEM uh ree) — after much repetition, muscle groups grow accustomed to specific motions

overtraining (O ver TRAYN ing) — the practice of ignoring the body's need for rest and recuperation after vigorous training

GLOSSARY

physiologist (FIZ ee AHL uh just) — one who studies the biological science of life processes, activities, and functions

protein (PRO TEEN) — a complex nitrogenous compound containing amino acids; it is essential for the growth and repair of animal tissue

quad stretches (KWAD STRECH ez) — a warm-up exercise designed to loosen the quadriceps, the muscles in front of the thigh

slow twitch fibers (SLO TWICH FIE berz) — rich in blood, these muscular fibers aid in long-distance, endurance events

stamina (STAM uh nuh) — (like endurance) the ability of an individual to resist the effects of fatigue

static stretching (STAT ik STRECH ing) — holding a stretched position for a count of five or more (as opposed to bouncing)

tendon (TEN dun) — a band of tough, non-elastic fibrous tissue connecting bone to muscle

toe touches (TO TUCH ez) — a warm-up exercise designed to loosen the hamstrings

trunk twisters (TRUNK TWIS terz) — a warm-up exercise focusing on the spinal vertebrae

FURTHER READING

Find out more with these helpful books and information sites:

Kirschmann, Gayle J. (contributor) and Kirschmann, John D.
Nutrition Almanac (4th edition), McGraw-Hill, 1996

Koch, Edward R. *USA Track and Field Directory,* USATF, 1993

Peterson, Marilyn S. *Eat to Compete: A Guide to Sports Nutrition,*
Mosby, 1996

Smith, Nathan J., et al. *Kidsports: A Survival Guide,* Addison-Wesley,
1983

American Track and Field Online at
www.runningnetwork.com/aft/

M-F Athletic Company at
www.mfathletic.com (an online catalog for track and field books,
tapes, clothes, etc.)

Track and Field News at
www.trackandfieldnews.com/

United States of America Track and Field at
www.usatf.org

INDEX